Margie

VICTIM
OF MEDICAL NEGLIGENCE

JERRY BROWN-SARRE

Published in Australia by Sid Harta Publishers Pty Ltd,
ABN: 46 119 415 842
23 Stirling Crescent, Glen Waverley, Victoria 3150 Australia
Telephone: +61 3 9560 9920, Facsimile: +61 3 9545 1742
E-mail: author@sidharta.com.au

First published in Australia 2019
This edition published 2019
Copyright © Jerry Brown-Sarre 2019
Cover design, typesetting: WorkingType (www.workingtype.com.au)

The right of Jerry Brown-Sarre to be identified as the Author of the Work has been asserted in accordance with the Copyright, Designs and Patents Act 1988.

The Author of this book accepts all responsibility for the contents and absolves any other person or persons involved in its production from any responsibility or liability where the contents are concerned.

All rights reserved. No part of this publication may be reproduced, stored in a retrieval system, or transmitted, in any form or by any means without the prior written permission of the publisher, nor be otherwise circulated in any form of binding or cover other than that in which it is published and without a similar condition being imposed on the subsequent purchaser.

Brown-Sarre, Jerry
Margie: Victim of Medical Negligence
ISBN: 978-1-925230-57-4
pp130

ABOUT THE AUTHOR

Jerry Brown-Sarre was Margie's husband

And he is the father of their two sons and grandfather to 8 children from their two sons.

He was inducted into the Australian Road Transport Hall of Fame in 2005

With a Diploma of Law and as an expert in Road Transport issues, and now retired, he spends his time continuing to try and help prevent the unnecessary daily deaths of transport drivers, something he started with Margie in 2000.

At the same time, trying to get people to understand their rights in medical malpractice deaths and injuries, with the hope that other people will not have to go through what he and his family did, and to point them to lawyers who can help them get justice.

While he doesn't drive any more, he still follows his favourite motor sport of Sprintcar Racing

To Margie

Margie

This is your life story.
As mother and a wife your story is
about a woman who survived anything
life in general put to you.

But you didn't plan on the challenge
of medical negligence to test you.

CHAPTER ONE

Day 1

It is 2.30 pm, my head is spinning, still in shock, listening to the vascular surgeon's words, your wife's left leg has necrosis, after 18 hours of lack of blood because of a tear in the femoral artery that wasn't managed properly by the previous hospital.

He has told me you have 2 choices, amputation above the knee, or leave it alone and she will die in a matter of hours.

Warning me, If we do amputate, at her age, she only has a 20% chance of surviving because of the tension pneumothorax, toxic shock, bad vital signs, and low oxygen saturations that she is has.

I am at one of the leading trauma hospitals in Melbourne where she has been flown from a large Victorian regional hospital for emergency vascular surgery.

Twenty eight hours ago I called an ambulance to take her to the local regional hospital after she collapsed at home after she had not been feeling well because of a flu virus for two days.

The Emergency Department doctors at the hospital had then diagnosed her with severe pneumonia.

They said following 3 days in the Intensive care unit she would be ok and back home.

Two days earlier she was perfect and healthy and I told those doctors they had to fix her, she can't die.

At 2.00 pm I kissed her and said she must stay in hospital to get well and I would back at night with the boys to see her. She asked were me for a drink of water before I went and complained that her arms were sore.

I knew it was serious and I worried if would it be the last time she would talk to me.

But she was already looking better after receiving oxygen and some other drugs so I was confident she would be right in a few days.

I then made a mistake and entrusted them with her life.

At 7 00 o'clock that night the family and I had turned up at the hospital to see her, where they refused to let us see her saying that she was in serious condition with a collapsed lung.

I demanded to see her and they finally consented, there

were no answers then why the lung had collapsed, and now more questions.

The phone call came from the hospital at 6am next morning saying she must be transferred to a Melbourne hospital because she has a blockage of the femoral artery,
My response to the nurse was, what, how ? She only has the flu how can that effect her arteries.

I arrived at the hospital just as they were taking her to the ambulance and tried to get answers from doctors what had happened to her, they just ignored me.
How did her lung collapse? How did the femoral artery get blocked? What has this got to do with pneumonia? Your mind is full of constant questions with no answers.
I'm just a transport driver I don't know the meaning of all these medical terms they are using, but that will change. She would have known the meanings of the words, but I can't ask her.
To everyone who knew her, she was simply, *Margie*.

Her model pose, how can I amputate that leg?

CHAPTER TWO

This is now the biggest decision of my life, the doctors want a decision now, amputate or not? I don't know what to say.

The last time a life or death decisions was made in our family it was by her in 1974 when I had collapsed 200 kilometers from Melbourne with a gangrene contaminated gall bladder.

No ambulances were available and she had to drive there on her own to pick me up, and return to a northern Melbourne private hospital for emergency surgery

I remember waking up at one point and seeing the speedometer in the Falcon GT HO hovering around the 100mph and saying to her, just be careful.

Then the surgeon telling me I had been close to death and the time saved getting me to surgery had been crucial.

Luckily, I trusted her driving skills; she was a confident

driver after driving all my high performance cars we had owned over the years.

She saved my life then, now it's my turn, can I do it for her?

I remembered the last time I had this fear and dread in the pit of my stomach thinking I was going to lose her.
This is her left leg, how would she respond, this beautiful, independent woman whose long legs were a major part of her life, those years in bikinis, mini-skirts, dancing, at the beach, as hosiery model, as air hostess ,always active. Would she hate me, would she rather die than finish her life as cripple?

This is not a decision I should have to make,ever.

Even at over 70 she kept her golden tan with some sun bathing, she still wore a bikini and mini-skirts, and still looked fantastic with those long tanned legs, I loved them.

Through the fog I hear the doctors talking to me, I'm having trouble concentrating.

Time demands an answer.

I finally said, amputate, hoping it will keep her alive, and it would be the right decision and sign the consent form.

Then the agonizing phone calls to tell our sons who are still in disbelief because of what's happening to their mother.

I remember thinking, is this being selfish and just for me? Am I thinking of her quality of life, I dismissed the thoughts.

I need her to live and I will do whatever it takes.

The 9 hour wait to get the results seems like forever just thinking what I have just had to do.

I'm not a religious person but for the first time in my life I prayed that night, it was time to get help from anywhere.

Sitting in the waiting room on my own I started to remember her life, our life…

CHAPTER THREE

She was about 63 and came home from shopping all chuffed and saying, I must still have it, some guys at a building site gave me wolf whistles, she said I waved and got more whistles, and then she laughed

It used to happen all the time when she was younger.

Why don't feminists and other women of today like that type of compliment?

A mother of 2 children, who still basically had the same body as she had when we met over 48 years ago, except the 19 inch waist was now 22 inches.

She made her own black cocktail dress when we went to Smacka Fitzgibbons nightclub in the late 60s and only a couple of years ago wore the same dress to her son's wedding.

A feat most woman would like to be able to do.

I particularly liked her wearing her white Marilyn Monroe

dress or her white tasseled roaring twenties dress, but then also, she could fill out a pair jeans or slacks really well.

Unlike today's independent women with the time and money and the need to go to the gym 2 or 3 days a week, get cafe lattés every day with their girlfriends, or purchase memberships with one of the many weight loss programs.

She simply said, you can stay healthy and fit by looking after your own family and your home.

Only saying on the morning she got sick that she weighed 62 kgs. It was a weight where she felt comfortable at that time of her life.

Before I met her, she was going out with well-off boyfriends who had money to impress her.

She liked all the popular alcoholic drinks of the time but, after meeting me, a non drinker of any type of alcohol, she stopped and will now only drink alcohol when we go to parties.

She doesn't need it, not with such a natural beauty.

She has a smile which would light up a room, a smile that can transform my bad day into good day just by looking at her .

She lost her baby weight within about 2 months each time of giving birth to our two sons.

However she was like all women in thinking her body

A smile that would make your day

wasn't perfect and she needed to be told it is perfect, which I have done for 49 years.

The one thing she liked about being pregnant was how her boobs grew and didn't need to add socks in her bra when were going out.

When they returned to normal size each time I would console her by saying, your boobs are perfect for me, it made her laugh and forget about it .

CHAPTER FOUR

My mind goes back to when we met over 48 years ago when I was a 19 year old boy from the other side of the tracks, she was a 24 year old girl from a middle class family, and we were complete opposites.

On the day we met, completely by chance, both of our lives would change forever.

It was 1961, a warm September day, I had agreed to help a new friend move some rubbish from another new friend's parent's house in northern Melbourne suburb.

I was a rev head of the times in my 1952 Ford Twin Spinner, basically all that I owned, and I was in shares with a finance company with it.

As I walked past the kitchen window to get to the back yard at the house unbeknown to me I had been seen by my mate's sister.

She had seen a man with dark skin who she didn't know walk past the window and had run to her bedroom to take out the curlers and put on relevant clothes to suit the day.

All that took was shorts and a top and it was enough to basically have a sticky beak, and find out who it was.

After introductions I found out it was the home of a mate who I had been hanging around with for a couple of weeks.

I also found out at that time after I saw this tall, sun-tanned blonde, come out from the house in those short shorts, with those long legs, that he had a sister.

She was gorgeous, and I immediately decided I had to take her out and get to know her.

After completing the work of cleaning up and taking loads to the tip we went back to the house for a drink.

Sitting at that kitchen table with this gorgeous woman where she was repeatedly refusing my request for a date, I was transfixed by her beauty.

She was continually arguing the 5 year age difference was too great and people would think she was cradle snatching.

I argued it was only 4 years 9 months and I didn't care what people said or thought.

It took me 3 hours to get her to agree for the date, which was to go to the drive in theatre, followed by a country drive to the top of Mt Pretty Sally looking at a view of Melbourne at night while dining on a pie with sauce and a bottle of coke.

The day we met, I don't have the 6 pack now unfortunately
She carried this photo in her wallet for 48 years

We would do this drive many times over the following years.

It would not have worked with women of today, go to a drive in theatre and a pie and a coke for a date.

Imagine how they would react, with no glasses of red.

I have found a lot of women of today are pretty shallow.

A second date next day, and every day thereafter was the start of a relationship that would last the rest of our life.

Its 11.30 pm when the surgeons finally came out to tell me that the surgery has been done, she is in an induced coma and she is recovering. Now we wait.

She is in Intensive care and confined to single room until they find out what caused the chest infection.

I was advised there was nothing I could do now but wait, the next 48 hrs are crucial, so I should go home.

I knew I could now relax because I was confident she was finally in the best care I could give her.

For the whole 2 hour drive home all I could think of was whether this was my fault, should I have taken her to hospital sooner?

Should I have taken her to a different hospital knowing the problems that this hospital reportedly had, according to the news reports by patients with allegations of negligence?

… *Chapter four*

Day 2

The next morning I was still in shock I checked with the Melbourne hospital ICU, nothing has changed, she is stable, still in the coma, I decided she doesn't need me down there yet, I'll go later.

I made an appointment with the ICU registrar at the country hospital where it started; I wanted answers with regards to what happened

I arrived for the appointment and I was ambushed by doctors using medical terms to tell me it was not their fault, they were clearly in a panic.

I remembered the saying "thou does protest too much", so I decided that I will need to investigate just what happened. Clearly they are hiding something.

I drove to Melbourne, sat with her, talk to her, hoping she could hear me, hoping she wakes up, she didn't.

If only the hospital beds were wider, I would stay here and sleep with her.

The waiting continues.

CHAPTER FIVE

Day 3

I Drove to Melbourne from country Victoria, the two hour drive each way that I would do every day, would be the time to remember our life.

A second date next day and every day thereafter was the start of relationship that would last the rest of our life.

After the second date her parents are not happy.

I'm from a lower class suburb in those days, and they have already found out from my mate, their younger son, about my low class job as a truck driver, where I live, I don't have any money, also, with a dark tanned skin they think I'm Aboriginal.

I definitely don't fit the criteria for their daughter; this wasn't going to happen as far as they are concerned.

Her parents were domineering, from old English heritage dating back to the times of the Baskervilles on her mother's side and even though she was 24 years old, they still had control over her, and unfortunately, out of respect for them or maybe love, she allowed herself to be controlled by them.

I made the assumption out of respect and love, I never found out why she let them treat her like that.

Her father, born in England from upper class English family, was a former flight sergeant in the air force during the war, his father the original owner of the Bell Street Bus Company in Melbourne.

Her mother, whose parents were also from England, was born in Mansfield Victoria, whose father ran a clothing company in Melbourne.

She was a former Sunday school teacher both of them were religious but not practicing.

Her mother raised her children by herself during the war while her husband was overseas.

Maybe it was the Catholic religion or the country upbringing that made them continue to control their children.

Somewhere in that upbringing was the mindset coming from an England based family, where the children stayed in the family home until they got married under the control, intimidation and forced love of the parents,

I remember taking a daughter of a religious sect leader out on a date, even they weren't that strict.

This control was held over their two oldest children and that would last longer than was normal.

Margie was put on a pedestal by her father and such; it was instilled in her not to do anything he wouldn't like ever. While her mother was the enforcer who made sure everyone did what they were told as long as you lived in her house.

It never worked on my mate the youngest son, who simply rebelled against the power, but the siblings were very close with a strong bond between them.

Not starting out good, I could tell they weren't happy about me but I was used to that from parents of girls, but she was a young woman, this situation was different.

She later told me she fell in love with me when she first met me and after wouldn't give up on asking her out, we never spoke of the age difference again.

Day 4

I drove the two hour drive to the hospital, her condition is stable, and there is still hope, still in a coma.

I held her hand and then notice the black and red wounds over her arms.

I counted them, 53 wounds in total, I called the nurse and ask her what caused them and I'm told they happened at the county hospital and were caused by attempted cannulation of the arteries in her arms.

I recalled watching these incompetent emergency department doctors at the country hospital trying to insert a arterial central line in her arms in order to give her antibiotics, everyone on the room having turns to locate an artery and all failing.

She had told me her arms were sore, now I know why.

I realised that further attempts must have continued after I left the hospital and her in their care, even after telling me they were waiting for an arterial doppler to help them place the line in the right place

Continuing trying to cannulate arteries without assistance after 3 failed attempts, it is considered to be criminal assault.

In Queensland where it is statute law under the health act, after 3 attempts to locate an artery and none can be found, an arterial doppler must be used to locate the artery, and doctors can only cannulate the right lung, what happened to her, this would be assault.

In Victoria it's simply considered just grossly incompetent not to use an arterial ultrasound to assist if the patient is dehydrated and arteries cannot be found.

Not making sure you don't cannulate the good lung because of the foreseeable possibility of a tension pneumothorax, this is just common assault.

I stayed with her all day in case she wakes up; I have to be the one to tell her what I did to save her life, hoping that she will forgive me.

Her vital signs and saturations remain stable; I drove home again..

CHAPTER SIX

After Margie left school at 16, she started a hairdressing course, after some months she decided she didn't like hair dressing.

However, she would do all the family haircuts, perms, including her own forever because of hair dressing skills she obtained, not that she always wanted to, but it's now her job to all the family even doing my hair cuts for 48 years.

She then started work as chemist dispensary sales person where she would work for 10years, the money was crap, but it was a family business and she liked the family that owned it

At 5,11 135 lbs she had a waist of 19 inches ,she was a striking blonde with a love for hair styles of movies stars of the forties, Hedy Lamar, Ginger Rodgers, Susan Heyworth, Lauren Bacall, and the like.

In early days her hair was worn short later long and only needed and used the most basic make up except when going out somewhere special with me, then she would spend more time on her hair and more time on make up around her eyes.

Having a natural beauty like a lot of gorgeous young women, as they age they get a more mature beauty, which comes from inside and that was her, to me, more beautiful at 70 than she was at 24 and I told her that often.

Newspapers and TV shows are all about what we called the beautiful people of the world, who spend a fortune to keep themselves looking young, and a lot still *don't* succeed,

You need the basic genes to start with, she had it.

I told her, when she reached 50 and older, to me, she changed to a more mature more natural beauty which came from the inside.

Not every young woman will achieve that mature beauty at 50 and above.

You see it in photos of the older beautiful people of the world, no matter how much money they spend on themselves, only special ones succeed in keeping or gaining that beauty.

When I met her, she was an actress Mitzi Gaynor look alike; *South Pacific* being one her favorite movies, she called me her Tony Curtis look alike.

When she walked into room when she was young, and

My Mitzi Gaynor

even now, she stood out because of her height, the way she dressed and how she carried herself, with that blonde hair and that smile.

It was a time of innocence and naivety; there were no drugs around except in the strip clubs.

It was before the disco nightclubs were set up, before the woman's liberation movement.

In the 70s, flower power and Woodstock started the ban the bra and the current free sex revolution.

It would become later, a way of life for young women and men of the world.

She was from a time when most women had more respect for themselves than they do in our modern society of feminism, and waited for and until the right man came along, hopefully.

She studied ball room dancing at Arthur Murray and went dancing every night that she could.

There was dancing at the various town halls around Melbourne in those days.

Her dance cards were always full, but going home with someone was controlled by her big brother who accompanied her and who decided under instructions from her parents whether she could come home with anyone else.

She even also taught dancing for a while at the studio.

Chapter six

Her brother said she was the best dancer he had ever danced with.

And then there was also dancing at the various nightclubs where her well off boyfriends would take her over the years.

CHAPTER SEVEN

Day 5

I drove down to Melbourne when the doctors told me she is coming out of their self induced coma and her vital signs and saturations are improving.

The nurses explain her vital signs and her oxygen saturation levels are monitored 24 hours a day and they tell us by simply looking at the computer monitor that she is hooked up to with numerous leads and hoses that it shows how she is responding to her management.

I have told them not to tell her what has happened till I get there.

After this news I'm on a high.

When I see her with tubes everywhere and now has a new tracheal intubation fitted so she can't talk, out of the coma, still highly drugged, but alive.

I don't have the courage to tell her then what I had to do to save her and decide to tell her the next day.

That day I had sent a freedom on information request to the country hospital for all her files and I was waiting to find out and to understand what had happened.

Looking at her I am reminded of our past.

She saved up every year for an annual holiday to the Gold Coast, she loved the sea she loved the beach and the sun, all her life.

In 1961 she told me she had the tickets and reservations to go to the Gold Coast for her annual holiday, but didn't want to go now she has met me.

I told her to go and enjoy her holiday I would still be here waiting.

Two years earlier she was caught in a rip at Kirra beach on the Gold Coast but had been saved by life guards.

She eventually went out with one of the life guards a few times before coming home that year.

She booked an apartment close to the ocean each year, sharing with a couple of girls she had met her first year there.

That particular year 1961, she would meet a millionaire, who later would become a member of the gold coast white shoe brigade of millionaire property owners who would develop the gold coast in later years.

He flew her to his alleged own major tourist island resort in his own plane, took her out to nightclubs and wanted her to come to the gold coast to live together with him.

He promised he would give her an apartment to live in, give her a job and a car.

But really it would just a scam by him to get into her pants, and after he told her he was married, she knew it, and the promise of money was not going make it happen.

She untimely declined saying she was in love with a truck driver back home.

A typical rich dude they will say anything and use their money to impress young women to get what they want.

Every night clubs at the time would have nightly or weekly limbo competitions. She won many of them she was so fit and agile. It was a time when you didn't need drugs and alcohol to enjoy life, being alive itself was the drug.

Day 6

On the way down to the Melbourne hospital I tried to prepare what to say to her.

It is another high day she is looking better, I checked the monitor, her vitals and saturations are good, and this will be the first thing I check every time I come to see her.

The doctors tell me to prepare that she won't survive, but I refuse to believe that, she has to survive I need her.

She is out of the isolation ward, she knows me, but can't speak, but still mouths the words, I love you, three times. How am I going to tell her what I did?

I can tell she is confused to where she is and why she is there, so I told her that the local hospital stuffed up big time. But I will I find out what they did and we will make them pay.

I told her she has been very sick, and that I had to make the biggest decision of my life so I could keep her alive and that I hoped she would forgive me.

I also told her she has been very brave and I am proud of her but she is going to have to fight to get better.

She must not give up, that I will be with her too and will be there to help her every day, but I didn't have the guts to tell her what I had to do.

Instead telling myself, that's ok that I'll tell her tomorrow.

On the way home again I continued to remember the past.

She had been engaged twice, before I met her, breaking up with the last one, 12 months earlier because she didn't like his family, another one because she didn't like his feet, other relationships for relative minor silly reasons, another because he wasn't a good kisser,

But really, they ended because they weren't right for her and it was her heart telling her to make up an excuse and she realised it before it was too late.

She said that she broke off the engagements and finished letting these blokes take her out, because, while she loved them one way or another.

She wasn't in love with them.

She would say. You can love your parents, a pair of shoes, the cat, or a dress, but getting married because you like someone or love them that day won't make for a long marriage.

She was a romantic, and said being in love with someone might only happen once in your life.

It is a feeling you get when in contact with special person, and she didn't know what it meant it until she met me.

A tingle in her hand, butterflies in the stomach when I walked in to the room, an empty feeling when I left her at the front door, excitement when I called on the phone, a feeling of being safe when she was with me, being her best friend, and most important butterflies when being kissed.

You must love the person as they are now, not what you want them to be she would say.

She told me not long before she got ill, that the feeling was still there, the butterflies when I kissed her goodbye before leaving to go on trip, after 48 years that's not bad.

Your eyes are the windows of the soul, they tell everything about you, so the saying goes…

I am but a mere male and It took me 48 years to recognise that if a woman is in love it will show in her eyes when you kiss them, as it did in hers every time I did.

CHAPTER EIGHT

Day 7

I drove down to the hospital, this is not a good day, her vitals and saturations are down, and there are complications due to infection with the left leg.

Again I still don't tell her what I had to do.

Then they asked consent to remove a further 4 inches of the limb.

This raises a problem; there was just enough of the limb to have a **prosthesis** fitted, now with the shorter limb she will most likely have to be confined crutches or to a wheel chair for the rest of her life.

She will hate losing her independence.

I told them to do what they had to fix the problem; I dreaded having to tell her this news.

I waited until after the 6 hour operation then I drove back home again in a depressed mood, thinking of our life.

Any one of the previous boyfriend's had her parents blessing but it didn't matter once she made up her mind on this point.

Her boyfriends over the years before meeting me consisted of, an accountant, a policeman, a big name international sports star, a doctor, business men, even a transport driver who she found out was married before dumping him .

She could have lived a comfortable life with the rest of them had she been in love with them or simply said yes, something a lot of woman do.

The transport driver would try to come back in to her life 30 years later after meeting him through speedway with me, but she soon gave him short shift when he stated harassing her for a catch up date, but not before telling me what he was up to.

She would mention many of them later over the years, seeing them in newspapers articles and stories.

Except for one long time on an off again boy friend, who she met when she was 17 and was a dancing partner .

He asked her to marry him many times but she kept rejecting him because that special magic wasn't there.

CHAPTER NINE

Day 8

Before driving down to the Melbourne hospital I went to the meeting with the country hospital complaints personnel to find out more about her negligent management.

I was treated like a mushroom, kept in the dark and fed bullshit with all the medical terms and excuses for what happened to her and no admittance of their fault by the surgeon all though at a full meeting of management the ICU HMO had conceded "we could have done better for her."

But I now know more after receiving the records of her management, which show incompetence and negligence and bias of age by the doctors who were in charge of her management.

I still don't understand the medical terms but it will now be my challenge every night to Google every word to understand the meanings, something all relatives of the sick should do: ask questions.

I drove down to the Melbourne hospital again hoping for better news, she is awake but drowsy, but she knows what has happened to her by hearing her doctors talking in their morning rounds.

She is not happy and I can tell. All I can say to her is that I love her and I will look after her,.

I stay with her, but it is a depressing down day.

Her vitals and saturations are down, but she is looking a bit better, as I sit with her I remember more of the past.

I decided to engage solicitors to act for her but they need to specialise in medical negligence as my enquiries have told me it is a specialty area of law.

Therefore not part of my current studies that I'm doing working towards a diploma in law.

I will have to change my legal studies to concentrate on medical negligence and find a legal firm who will work with me to get her justice for the loss of her leg.

She was looking for that special person, the love that had to be out there for her.

She kept herself pure for that person out of self- respect for herself, and her future husband when she found him.

Respect for yourself and others was something she felt

Ready for another dance

very strong about, everyone had their own choice for their own body she would say.

When I met her and even later in life she was extremely careful what language she used in the company of others.

She believed that you should keep respect for yourself, and set your own boundaries, and women should not lower or degrade themselves in company.

Like dropping the F bomb and especially the C bomb, a word that I never heard her use ever , in company.

Her old fashioned ideas are not supported by the majority of today's women especially the young and in particular feminists. She was trying to instill the same values into her two Granddaughters; I can only hope she was successful.

She acted, dressed and talked like a lady you could take anywhere.

Her actions were always based on respect for her-self which affected those around her, including me.

While it is not considered important by many young women today, but with the boyfriends she had gone out with, she had decided for her own self-respect not to be sexually active with any one until she fell in love.

I was luckily that person that would finally unlock that door for her sexual awakening, a privilege I never abused out of respect for her.

She would tell her boyfriends how far the romance could go, and luckily for me and her, it was a time when men and boys knew what that meant and respected that.

She would often tell me of embarrassing moments for some of the guys while dancing or doing other things and having a giggle about it.

CHAPTER TEN

Day 9

I drove down to Melbourne, she has had the family in to see her and her vital signs and saturations are up and hopefully things are improving.

I stayed with her for the day.

The hospital is talking of removing the tracheal tube and moving her to a general ward.

I can't wait for her to have proper food so she can get her strength back and use her arms and talk to me.

I remember after that first weekend we met, we were inseparable spending all our time together and with others, much to the disagreement of her parents.

We are together for 9 months, doing everything together just having fun.

Her father always said she was in love with love, and she was a romantic, which means holding hands while walking down the street, sitting with her at parties and not leaving her alone while the men go into a corner and talk, the romantic kind of things that romantics and maybe most women want.

And while she could have lived the life of luxury with most of the other long term boyfriends she had been involved with.

She decided a life of adventure and the unknown with someone she loved was how she wanted to live her life, that said, she, we, didn't know how hard a struggle life would be at times.

I had stopped boarding and moved into a flat with the mates in a northern suburb. I would be closer to her meaning we could have more alone together time.

Her young brother lasted a couple of months then moved back home to his mother to do his washing and cooking. Then our other mate moved back to his home.

As I couldn't afford the flat on my own I had to move out and find new boarding digs.

We were young, virile and naive in not using protection and it was inevitable that the day in May would come, the statement that many young couples hear, I'm late, and so our lives changed forever.

Day 10

The hospital was concerned with her failing internals and kidney problems.

The lung is healing and her leg has stabilized so we continue to watch hope and pray.

It was frustrating not being able to tell her what happened to her and why she was in hospital because I just didn't understand at that time what had taken place.

The two hours each way driving down and back gives me more to time remember parts of our life.

We decided after getting a positive confirmation from a doctor there would be no abortion and that we would get married. However family problems with that idea arose and shocked us.

It was time to tell her parents the news we were going to get married and or we would live together until I was old enough if my father would not give consent for a license. I got an unexpected reaction to that request. In 1962 in Australia if you were under 21 you needed parents consent to marry.

I went to my father to get the permission and to my surprise he said no saying that she just wanted to get married and she wasn't pregnant and she was trying to trap me into marriage.

He told me he would not be agreeing to me marrying her and generally abusing them and her, and then, without me knowing he rang Margie's parents and abused them for what he thought they were doing.

Even though I had been living away from home on my own since was 15 years old and never needed his permission or anything, this was the law at that time on this matter.

He thought he was looking after my future, how wrong he was.

It was shock to her family that this could happen to their only daughter with this no hoper truck driver, it would be acceptable if it was any of her previous boyfriends.

Her parents objected and told me to get out of the house and never come back and never contact her again.

They prevented her from having any rights, and she wasn't allowed to leave the house and come with me,

It was like family imprisonment and that resulted in a major argument and altercation with members of the family by me.

That phone call my father made to her parents would be the catalyst her parents would use to get her to agree not to see me and for her to do as they wanted.

I didn't know about the phone call for a long time and I wasn't happy he stuck his bib in.

Next day I rang her at work, she wasn't there and I tried every day for a week until they told me she was on sick leave and in hospital.

She was not allowed to answer the phone as I found out when I rang the house to find out what was happening to her.

I went to the house to talk to her when her father threatened me with a shovel and told me to leave her alone, more angry words spoken.

I didn't know what hospital she was at but I eventually got a letter from her.

She told me that her parents took her to a different doctor who said she wasn't pregnant she only had an ovarian cyst which they operated on and removed.

Day 11

She is still stable, still hope, so I sit with her, talk to her and remember more, this was Australia,1962.

She was 25 years old and they couldn't stop her doing whatever she wanted, could they?

They did that day, but they couldn't prevent the inevitable.

I was concerned at this time, with nothing to bind us together now, and the pressure from her family not to let her see me would it all be over between us?

The only bond we had was that I was her first lover, but would it be enough?

Margie rang me from a phone box to where I was boarding to give me a heads up that her brother and her old dance boy friend were coming to my place to give me a bashing for taking advantage of his sister.

When they got there I told them not to start what they can't finish and stay out things that don't concern them.

Her hypocritical brother would poke anything with legs, no matter whose sister or wife it was.

CHAPTER ELEVEN

A while later, a used car dealer next to her work kept asking her out, he was part of a group of friends of her brother, she asked me if she should.

I said she could if she wanted to, it would let her parents think we weren't in contact, so she told him she would go out with him, but not to expect anything serious.

He would take her to night clubs, and on weekend outings. She would tell me where he was taking her, I wasn't happy, but then it was out of my hands.

However this would lead to secret meetings.

She would tell me of certain motor bike racing events or football matches he was taking her to. Naturally I would happen to be here.

I would turn up casually after she would tell me, where and when, I even met them at the movies some times.

He didn't know me and our history, and I would stand behind her and hold her hand without him noticing, nearly got caught a couple of times, it was worth the risk.

Sometimes she would ring me and ask me what was on nearby and she would then get him to take her there so we could meet.

She finally told him she was going to stop seeing him because she was in love with someone else.

We had decided her parents would not stop us from seeing each other even though her brothers were given the job of following her and reporting back if they saw her with me.

This naturally made it hard to see each one and other, her father would pick her up from work and I couldn't ring her at home, so it was hard to stay in direct contact with her.

Her parents forced her to let her old dancing partner take her out after she had stopped seeing the used car sales man.

She had rang me and asked me what to do, I said do what they want, they will think they are winning

Margie's old dance friend was told what had happened by her parents and started asking her out, after a few weeks he asked her to marry him, again, and again she said no.

She told him not to come around anymore after he starting putting the hard word on her, something he had never done previously.

I had started taking out a girl I met at the Melbourne

show at that time while she was going out with these blokes, it would only last a few weeks it was never going anywhere.

I think I only did it because I was jealous of her dating other blokes.

Her brother kept telling Margie and her parents what I was doing, and when she found out I was taking this girl out she rang me at home, she was very jealous, asking me if I was serious with this blonde haired bitch, I told her I wasn't, and I had stopped seeing her and I never used her name in front of her again.

She told me then she had been faithful to me since we were made to break up and we had to do something to get back together.

We agreed to start seeing each other again somehow, so maybe it was a good thing she found out.

I got jealous of all this crap and told her we had to stop and that we have to take on her father and mother.

But she was under her parents control somehow and couldn't go through with it.

We would still tell each other where we were going either over the phone by me ringing her at work or through letters to her work. She would ring me at my home all the while her parents thought they had won.

Around this time I had started picking her up after work

and driving her home making sure to drop her around the corner from her place.

Then she made arrangements with a work friend that we would meet at her friend's place which was a few streets away from her home. I would park my car even further away and walk there.

It would only happen for a short time a couple of nights per week .It wasn't ideal but a vast improvement over what it had been, 5 minutes here and there, we had to make the most of it.

This went on for some months until it came to a head one night after meeting her at her friends place.

I was walking back to my car when I saw Margie's older brothers' car driving slowly after me.

I stopped him and told him to mind his own business to leave her alone and let her get on with own life after all she was nearly 26 years old.

Later that night he went home to his parents and told them he had enough of this stupidity and that they should allow her to make her own decisions in life.

CHAPTER TWELVE

For 9 months they had tried to keep us apart but we beat them. I still wasn't allowed in their house but she told them she would continue to see me if she wanted, they now realised that they couldn't stop us seeing each other.

Some weeks went by and I received an invitation to dinner, the evening was full of pretty ordinary conversations, but we got through it, was this finally the acceptance we had longed for?, Perhaps not ,but it was the start of a civil relationship with them.

But we were back together and going steady for another 12 months. However if we went away for a weekend her mother would want to come as a chaperon, that didn't work out well.

I started racing speedway cars later that year, which I did for a couple years before selling the car..

It gave us another interest and she was my no 1 fan.

In early March 1964, 31 months after we first met, just before my 22nd birthday and 3 months before her own 27th birthday we sat in my car and took the next step.

I didn't need permission now.

I asked her. Do you want to marry a truck driver and race car driver; her response took all of 2 seconds.

Yes. When and how soon can we do it?

I remember thinking; this will really piss her parents off.

Day 12

I was driving down to the hospital again when the hospital rang telling me the ICU registrar needs to talk to me as soon as possible.

They informed me that I should think about turning off the life support as she is not responding as well as they would like.

I said no, it wasn't happening; a heated discussion, after this the hospital asked the same question every day.

That day the hospital told me they need to operate urgently that they have uncovered that her small bowel is blocked, they need permission to operate, so again I said yes.

Christ almighty, I thought to myself, how much more of this negligence she has got to endure.

The doctor explains the cause, most likely lack of or impeded blood supply to the intestines for the time her femoral artery was torn.

It was in fact twisted and they had to remove a large section due to a buildup of gangrene.

I waited hours until the operation was over before heading home, they are hopeful they can get her vitals and saturations under control again

Before leaving I spoke to the hospital ICU registrar who told me that in the 5years in charge he has ever seen a patient including victims of car accidents come into ICU with the problems she has, and he was astounded at her will to continue to fight towards recovering.

From then on he is now asking her every day if she wants to continue with medication, and she continued to nod yes.

This brings on an argument from me that I am in charge of the decision to continue not him, and not her, in her condition.

This argument on my rights, her rights, is left unanswered, but I chose to study the law on it I when I go home.

Upon doing so I find out that, if they want to take charge of her health then they will need a court order.

This is another down day for her.

CHAPTER THIRTEEN

Another 2 hour drive home, 2 hours of remembering, that's all you can do, and try understand why.

We discussed why marriages fail, either through no give and take, or through the romance vanishing from the relationship because one or both people didn't work on saving it.

She said then, she would never have grey hair on her head as long as they sold blonde in a bottle.

That she would always keep herself as young as she could, and true to her word, she did just that every day to this day.

Even if I would be the only person who would see her on that particular day, she would do her hair and apply the little makeup she needed.

She always made the effort to keep the romance alive and to support our marriage; also, she would never think, or dress old.

You are, as young or old as you think and act, she would say it's the little things that today's women don't do to work on their marriage.

Some of her friend's marriages had failed and she had asked them the reason so that we wouldn't make the same mistakes.

She required respect, honesty, loyalty and trust, which she, believed were the four most important things for a relationship and for friendships.

As four of our former so called friends found out over the years after she told me they hit on her, they didn't expect her to tell me of their breach of trust given to them by me, this was important to her.

Long distance transport drivers have the largest marriage failures in Australia as a result of their time away from their spouse.

The man is tempted because he is missing his home, the wife might be tempted because of lack of attention from the husband, or perhaps boredom,

We had friends who set aside the same day every week for romance, their marriage failed.

She said when the romance goes, loves goes and the marriage goes.

We agreed to keep the romance at any cost.

She never looked more beautiful

Romance has to be spontaneous any where any time, How many rooms are there in a house? I can leave that to the imagination.

If I was leaving for an interstate trip the last thing we would do would be romantic and as soon as possible after coming home. We would always find time to be together, we would never go to sleep after an argument without agreeing to solve first, it even if it meant agreeing we were both at fault.

In those early days I was away from home for weeks on end.

Later in life only away 1 or 2 days at a time, and we adapted well to the times, why change a good idea if it's working. But when kids come it takes ingenuity to keep to plans. But if you try you can do anything.

She had a wicked sense humor.

I came home after trip one day after being married about ten years to find a brunette washing dishes in the kitchen. I thought my luck had changed, then she turned around and Margie was looking at me with her smile.

She said, I was worried by now you might tired of blondes and if you were thinking of having an affair then I want it to be with me.

I told her I only like blondes, but then, only one particular blonde and only one woman, you, no matter what colour your hair is.

Over the years when I came home she could be auburn, brunette, black or blonde and I wouldn't find out until I arrived home, it kept things interesting I can tell you.

She would only keep the colour for a week or so, before she would do it blonde again, with her deep tan any colour looked good.

A friend of ours also married to a transport driver said to her. Let's keep a record on the calendar how often we are romantic and at the end of the year we will see who wins.

I don't know who won but the friend came around one day and had a look on our calendar, and all she said with a smile was. You dirty bastards.

Takes a special woman to marry a transport driver as many transport driver's wives will attest too.

You needed in those days and even today, to be prepared to throw the kids into a car and travel hundreds of kilometers to pick their husband up when getting home from a trip, when especially working for country based bosses.

No mobile phones then, only telegrams or leave messages with relations with a time and a place to be picked up, not every home had a phone in those days.

Later when running your own business, she had to be prepared at any time day or night when asked to put the kids in the car to grab tools and parts out the shed and travel hundreds of kilometers to where the truck breaks down so it could be fixed.

She never complained once, she did whatever, whenever I asked or needed her to.

CHAPTER FOURTEEN

Day 13
....

I'm at the hospital again, she had a good night and is stable today, I talk and read the paper to her as we continue to wait. Feeling helpless I had to do something.

She would not like just lying there without looking the best she could for me and anyone who came, or who could see her.

I decided to apply her makeup and comb her hair, then I showed her in a mirror the finished result, she smiled, that's all I needed.

Then the drive home again.

You can over plan weddings; I would have been ok with a registry office after what we had gone through and I was surprised that her parents after all that they did wanted to take the trouble away from us. Guilty conscience?

Her mother and aunties arranged the wedding in 14 days, her mother, an ex dressmaker made the dress, and the ceremony was held in a church in Pascoe Vale, a northern suburb on a Friday night, the reception was at her parents' house.

Just family and a few friends, none of my parents were invited, but it went well.

There was no $30000 honey moon in those days.

Enough money for a night at a motel then back to the in laws for breakfast, then a country drive, the honeymoon will come later when there is money for it, it would be 20 years before we found time.

It was back to work on Monday morning for both of us.

Neither of us talking to my father after his outburst 18 months earlier again and she didn't talk to him or allow him to visit the house for 2 years.

I supported, and it showed her strength of conviction and character if she was wronged by any one.

Margie would be happy where the dress is these days;

It is a stand out as part of a large wedding dress collection by friends of ours.

Both families said our marriage won't last, especially considering the age difference, but we proved them wrong. We were, by all standards, a mismatch, she was intelligent and

This was one of her happiest days of her life

had she wanted or been able to go to university she could do anything she put her mind to.

Educated at inner suburban girl's school and a girl's Catholic school to merit standard, a real girl next door and tomboy, part of the normal middle class family.

Captain of the basket ball team, a champion school swimmer, also on the track and field team .

She played cricket with the family in the back yard, climbing trees, or whatever was exciting in the family week end holidays and activities with her 2 brothers.

It was a time before woman's the liberation movement and the fight for woman's rights, when the girls going to university were only for the truly ambitious, rich, and or members of the well off families.

All that most girls needed was a good education and a desire to find the job you enjoyed until you got married.

Playing in water again

CHAPTER FIFTEEN

Day 14

I spent the day at the hospital again no change, she is stable, that's ok tomorrow might be better, as a bystander you feel helpless; intensive care is a morbid place. I put her make up on again and every day after that.

It's all I can do for her now.

She loved the movies and she had an autograph book signed by movie stars, she dreamt of flying all over the world and finding romance out there like they do in the movies.

She went to see all the overseas artists that came out to festival hall, and had decided being an air hostess was the job she for her.

She often dreamt of being on a cruise ship and dancing on the promenade deck, like they do in the movies.

At the time of our first meeting she had finished her courses to be an air hostess for TAA and was waiting for the next hostess intakes.

It was something she had wanted to do since leaving school and then she met me that stuffed that dream.

She had originally been side tracked from her dream by the boyfriends, but after breaking up with her last fiancé, had finally decided to do it.

She would never take up the job because it would mean not being with me.

I wanted her to take the job but she defied me and said no, she was staying with me.

My family life was completely different to hers I was from a broken home and suffered under the step mother from hell who blamed me for her failures, she had thrown boiling water over me in one particularly heated argument, but hey, shit happens in life .

I was a complete opposite to all the boy friend's and people she was involved with at that time in her life, had she taken the job with TAA its certain that she wouldn't have enjoyed anywhere near the amount of success and familial love that we now enjoy.

Looking at her in that hospital bed reminded me again what this incompetence and negligence had done to this beautiful brave woman.

I remembered that night 24 years earlier, the last time when I had felt the fear in my stomach that I had lost her.

We had had a good day, after running 3rd in the Victorian sprint car title when we got a flat tyre on the car trailer and I pulled over to change the spare wheel.

Highway traffic was unusually very quiet that night, and I was kneeling next to the trailer putting the new wheel on and Margie was standing next to me with a torch.

The next thing I remember was the absolute darkness, no sounds, so quiet, nothing.

I was sitting on the edge of the shoulder of the road, I sat up and went to grab hold of the trailer and wasn't there. I called out to Margie, no answer; I called again, no answer, fear set in, where is she.

I tried to become accustomed to the dark, called again no answer.

What had just happened?

I made out the silhouette of the rear of the car trailer in the dark, then I saw the torch down the embankment in the bushes, it was still on, and I climbed down to get it.

I used the torch to look around while continually calling Margie's name.

Then I saw her, lying down the embankment, no movement, not answering.

I can remember the fear in my stomach, that she was dead, I had trouble walking to her, my legs wouldn't work.

I felt for a pulse, there was one, thank god.

I found the strength and carried her up the embankment and sat on the shoulder of the road with her head in my lap, for it seemed like eternity, but probably just minutes.

I was just hoping it wasn't serious, talking to her trying to see if she was injured.

Then, a voice out of the darkness, saying, is there any one there, are you all right?

At the same time the high beam headlights of car came over the crest of the rise and lit up the road and all around.

I saw 2 men standing there with a torch trying to slow down the oncoming car.

Then I saw a wrecked car across the highway 150 feet away, my F100 with the car and trailer 20 feet away down the embankment.

Margie started to wake up and come around as I figured out what had happened.

The car had run up the rear of the car trailer with such impact the concussion from it had blown me on my bum and blown Margie down the embankment with such force it knocked her out when her head hit the ground

She was bruised and sore but alive; neither of us till this day can remember the impact or the few seconds thereafter.

CHAPTER SIXTEEN

Day 15

While going down again to Melbourne, I spoke to the ICU nurse on the phone who told me Margie's vitals and saturations are up and she is stable.

It's a good day for her, she is still fighting, the nurse holds the phone to her ear so I can talk to her, looks a promising day, there's even talk to transferring her to general ward.

I can't wait for the tracheal tube to be removed so she can talk to me again, I miss her voice.

We made mistakes like most people in that 1st year of being married. But we learnt, and 18 months later we had our first son.

She took on a job at a hosiery firm and finished up modeling their stockings, her legs were used on all their packaging and advertising.

Then there was an offer to continue modeling clothes, it was a mistake for her not to accept the offers, she could have gone anywhere in that business.

With me being away from home and working, the responsibility was on her to raise our first son she was no longer working so she was able to devote her time to him and the house.

She had gotten used to me being away 5 days a week and sometimes more, driving long distance transport.

We were happy with our life and 3 yrs later we had another son, and in celebration, seeing as I had had enough of renting,

I decided to surprise her when she got out of hospital.

With three personal loans to make up the deposit I bought her our first new house in a northern suburb.

The look on her face when I showed her after picking her up from hospital was absolutely priceless.

Day 16

I'm at the hospital. her vitals and saturations are up and stable.

They are hopeful it might be a good day to get the tracheal tube out and move her to a general ward and it might be closer to bringing her home so I can look after her.

Not being able to talk was frustrating to both of us.

It was a good day, she was attentive. Tomorrow might be better, memories continue on the drive home.

In the same year that I bought our new house, I decided to start our own interstate transport business but knew we would need to do it together.

I only had 7th grade schooling and I needed her brains to run it and teach me all that she knew, and teach me she did, starting out with nothing there was only way to go, success

Interstate transport is a toxic and hard business subcontracting with prime contractors who don't want to pay you and who just want to use your business and the money they owe you to make them money.

When they do, it takes up to 120 days to get paid for the work you have done.

Over the next 45 yrs she would show the character and strength that is needed from a transport owner's wife.

It was an asset rich, money poor business then, and still is today.

She would learn to live, look after a house, raise children, educate a husband, while dealing with these large business parasites.

That's were the words that can only apply to women come from, multi tasking, men have trouble doing it.

She loved the sun and the water and camping out, so we

did in those years have good family time having a caravan and speedboat based at Lake Eppolock

Day 17

She is stable, we continue waiting for her to transfer to a general ward and prepare to come home I sat with her for the day and talked about family, read the paper.

We were married about 7 years and it was during that time I came home one day to find her crying,

I started to panic, and then she said, she had been carrying a secret with her for 7 long years and couldn't keep it any longer.

At this point I was expecting the worst, but it turned out her parents had forced her to have an abortion all those years ago and forced her to fabricate the story of a ovarian cyst operation.

She said that he would have been a boy, she named him Raymond, and she thought of him every day.

Every day she regretted not fighting with her parents to let her live her own life and denying me my rights to know what was happening.

She made me promise not to leave her and forgive her. I didn't blame her for what she did, I visualized her.

On her own, being intimidated and bullied by her parents, her mother especially, would have been like an attack dog.

I imagined her mother for days using that phone call that my father made to them to convince her that I wouldn't marry her, telling her she would have to be a single mother and that that she wouldn't be able to raise the baby on her own, and they won't support her, until she finally agreed to have the abortion.

I had to find self control in that moment, and after letting it sink in for a while, I forgave her for not telling me at the time, In fact actually proud she had the courage to finally tell me.

I still don't know if her 2 brothers were also part of the intimidation that went on then.

What I never forgave, was the deceit. Her parents who came to my house hundreds of times since that day and had never admitted to having contributed to the death of my son.

My relationship with Margie's father & mother from when we got married until they died was civil at best.

When they died, I supported Margie but I felt nothing for them after what they did before we were married.

For everyone's sake I'm glad I didn't know about the abortion while they were a live or when they died, I doubt whether I would have been able to control myself.

I still find it hard to understand how parents can have

that much control over their children, even though we know many do, however it's not how normal Australian families conduct themselves .

In today's society, it would be a crime of mental assault, bullying and other criminal offenses by her family.

I knew if I bought it up with her parents she would blame herself and despite everything she did love them.

So for her sake I said nothing, and as far as I know they never knew she told me.

What was particularly wrong was that they made her pay them back the cost of her forced abortion.

But I think it explained why she thought that is sacrosanct for a woman to have control over her own body and only her..

After that day, it was a huge burden off her shoulders, she couldn't change the past but she could have input into the future.

She would have given her life for her children or me.

She found some kind of an inner strength to stand up for herself and her family and devoted her life to her children, and me making sure she was always there if needed.

She would not let any other person make derogatory remarks about her family, only she could do that, but she carried the guilt of what they made her do forever.

She did not believe in the feminine revolution ideas of women doing without men in their life, or not accepting male chivalry, but she did believe in woman's rights and their responsibilities

She never accepted that any woman should be abused or intimidated by their partner and must stand up for themselves, and if I had been like that she would have been gone.

She abhorred domestic violence and that women should not stay with abusive men for any reason not even for their children and it was up to governments to help them.

Margie might have been compelled to do the wrong thing all those years ago but she made up for it in later life.

She believed that the role of a wife is to stand alongside your husband at all times and support him in his decisions.

That should take preference over everything, but that would depend, in her opinion, on whether you are in love with your husband or yourself, and if you are not prepared to support him in everything he does, don't get married.

She would have been however a supporter of the "me too' movement against violence against women of today.

Margie was a city girl, but I decided to take her and our kids out of the city and move to the country, a small town on a few acres build a new house on it to raise the kids.

It was a tremendous amount of work building a new

house, new sheds, wooden fences and everything else that was required.

She would work all day with me, then look after the house and family, never complain.

A few acres needed animals so I bought some palomino horses to set a up a horse stud, they were top of the line horses and we as family showed them at horse shows, and won many championship ribbons.

I was amazed at how much courage it took for this ex city girl to prepare our palomino stallion for shows when I wasn't home, stallions can be dangerous for any one, but she knw how to talk to him and them to earn his trust.

She would also prepare the mares so we could go to horse shows when I returned from trips without the worry of me preparing them.

The best test for a city girl was helping me when a mare giving a foal was having a breach birth.

After I asked her for help, she assisted me in turning the foal and to get the foal born alive and well.

She named him Beau James.

CHAPTER SEVENTEEN

Day 18

At the hospital, sitting with her, having one sided conversations just hoping she would pull through.

I remember the strength of character that she has shown in her life.

Her vitals and saturations are stable, they are worried about infections in the leg wound and her bowel wound. What worries me is what is known as fatal hospital infections. Golden staph and toxic shock, the longer you are in a hospital up goes the risk of the infection.

My mind wanders again.

While we are waiting to be paid for the work we are doing, and I'm away earning the money, she is at home, running the house, looking after kids, trying to collect money, answering creditor's phone calls, putting them off until we get paid, and learning how toxic small business is.

It doesn't help that we had a corrupt bank manager who falsified signatures to contracts that would hurt us later.

At one stage while I was operating a small fleet of trucks, no cash flow due to large companies not paying us, she could have packed up left then, and I would have understood, but instead she just said, it will get better.

We will just stick it out until then; the money owing doesn't help, as she found out when I was away one time.

A debt collector came calling, giving a shot gun cartridge with my name written on it to our 12 year son, saying pay now or else. That would frighten any one

Or the time when the 6ft 6 140 kg ex copper repo agent came calling, bashing on every window intimidating and bullying an innocent woman and children.

Again, she could have packed her clothes grabbed the kids and left. However the strength and courage of a woman who loved her family can never be underestimated.

Although after that, and after calling the local copper to ask him to look after them, and after I had words with both men about what would happen if it ever did happen again, I was confident she would be ok.

Transport is ruthless business and only the tough survive and she proved she was as tough as anyone I knew in the business.

Nothing stopped her, she would drive our son 360 kilometers a week to learn to play the drums, and she would drive him to his football games where ever they were.

And she was with him in the ambulance when he was 16, the day he was seriously hurt, so bad, he stopped breathing on the way to hospital, she sat with him in hospital for 2 days.

And when our oldest son rolled his car she was the one in between, so I wouldn't go mad at him.

We set up a video shop in a semi, large country town and our eldest son ran it while we lived in another town and she would drive the 300 kilometers per day to be with him for a whole 6 months.

Whenever I had doubts about anything I was doing, or wanted to do, she would simply say, you'll work it out. You always do, whatever you decide I'm with you.

When I got involved in transport reform I told her it would cost us money, she was fine with it and said that's ok, I'm here, becoming my proof reader on all my correspondence and simply just supported everything I did

Day 19

I rang the hospital on the way down, her vitals and saturations are just stable, that's ok.

I went down and sat with her, talked to her, hoping she had turned the corner and remembered more of our life.

She always said that the transport business was a feast or famine business, some months you are rich ,others you are poor, you just have to adjust, and when having a bad day, have a coffee, a smoke, or just have some time for each other, that fixes everything, I can attest to that .

Over the years prime contractors would go broke owing you thousands of dollars. When that happens you might have to sell your house to pay your bills, and then save to buy a new one.

We did that 5 times over 40 years, she never complained even though it hurt her, she just said, make sure I'm in my own house when we retire, which I have.

In the latter years we enjoyed more profitable years working for better companies who paid when required which meant she could enjoy life.

Taking the opportunity of going to Hawaii her favorite place, as well as, Daydream and Hayman island for holidays.

We even got the opportunity to take that honey moon finally, but she never bitched about it taking so long to happen.

She said *when we are making millions, we will spend millions; while we are making peanuts we will spend peanuts.*

Pity more people today didn't follow that advice.

She was loyal and when I decided to race cars again she was my most vocal supporter and crew member going to every race meeting with me and the boys.

Although she did go mad when at one time I bought a race car engine with the house saving money, but our romance could see us through anything.

She had that uncanny woman's intuition, if she met a business person she would tell me if they were genuine or not.

Make no mistake, every time I ignored her she would be proven right.

The most serious case was with an American company and an incompetent lawyer acting for us, which ultimately cost us over I million dollars.

Don't you hate that when women are always right.

All she said was, its only money and another house, we will start again; a wife must stand by her husband in the good and the bad days.

When I said at age 60 that I wanted to study law, I was sick of these companies ripping us off it can be impossible to find a competent lawyer to help to recover money owed and to fight government imposts that we have to occur to operate in the industry.

One incompetent lawyer had cost us over 100 thousand of dollars in losing a case he shouldn't have lost .

She arranged for me to do an online Diploma of Law course, and would help me with the studies when I was home.

In later life we did find two good country lawyers who helped us win some good cases, they are there; you just have to find them.

CHAPTER EIGHTEEN

I told her it's nearly time for me to retire from long distance transport after surviving 50 years in the most dangerous job in Australia, as recently stated by a University survey.

Most importantly 50 years of her worrying about me being in an accident while I was away and not able to come home after each trip.

Like the thousands of wives of long distance transport drivers, dreading the midnight phone call or the knock on the door in the early hours of the morning by a police officer.

Three times over the years I had major accidents, but I made sure I rang her before anyone else told her.

I am reminded of her answer to a reporter in the award winning documentary I did for SBS in 2000, called "Sweatshop On Wheels."

When she was asked by the reporter how you do feel when your husband is away on these long distance trips every week, her reply was.

"I don't breathe from when he drives out of the yard and until he drives back in the yard again and if the news reports about a truck accident I don't breathe until he rings me".

I decided it's time to let her breathe permanently again.

And I would finally be able to do more things together with her.

She would in conversation with friend a few weeks before getting sick, say that she would live in tent as long as I was with her, material things don't matter to her.

We started not to depend on transport for a living and diversified into a new business.

An automotive workshop our eldest son managing it and in which Margie could have more input into.

And then and another new house, without the pressure of people not paying us we would finally keep this one,

Day 20

It's been a good day she is awake, listening while I talk about what is happening with her boys and the business.

Chapter eighteen

We are still worrying about infections in the wounds especially Golden Staph, and sepsis.

Her mouth is dry; I rubbed her gums with water with the side of my finger after the nurse tried putting her dentures in her mouth dry and hurting her gums.

I told her it's time for me to go home; she held my finger firmly with her teeth shaking her head to say no, holding my finger with her teeth for 10 minutes, before finally releasing the pressure on the finger.

I'll be back tomorrow I told her, she nods and smiles, this is good progress.

I can't wait for tomorrow until she can talk to me again I miss proper conversations with her.

Why do they make hospital beds only one bum wide?

She and both our sons are fans of all the outer space films and believe in other life in the universe. And as such it was ironic to hear them all come home one night after visiting family 20 kilometers away with an unbelievable story.

There is a mountain range close to home where there have over the years been stories of "unknown objects" in the sky.

On this night driving home just after dusk an unidentified flying object flew metres above them in the car.

In his excitement my eldest son broke his finger on the windscreen when he pointed at it

It was only there for a minute then just accelerated and was gone in seconds.

When she reported it, the skeptics said it was impossible and no one believed them.

To this day they will swear what they saw and our young son who is a sign writer can draw what they saw.

She knows what they saw and doesn't care. who believes her, she believes they were chosen to see it.

Later in life when mysterious carbon circles appeared on our back lawn and again the skeptics tried to make up other reasons, she again said we have been chosen.

Myself, as a person who has seen the infamous northern Australia min min light, I believe her and the boys .

CHAPTER NINETEEN

Day 21

The phone rang while I was on my way down to Melbourne and the hospital tell me she had a bad night.

Her vitals and saturations were severely down she is not responsive and the time has come to let her go.

This as a shock after yesterday.

I'm not prepared for this, she was so good yesterday, something must have happened and I intend to find out, But I'm not agreeing to this I need answers fast.

How do you tell someone their 21 day fight for life that you made them do is over, that you are going to end their life?

How do tell her incompetent and negligent doctors and incompetent hospital practices have killed her?

How do you tell her how much she is loved, how do you tell someone, meeting her, marrying her, having her as mother of your children was the best thing that could have happened to you?

How do you tell her she was the perfect wife the perfect mother the perfect woman the perfect lover?

Well that's easy, when they are in a coma, you can think it but you can't and don't tell them anything. She doesn't deserve to die this way, this is uncompleted life she still has things to do.

I arrived at the hospital and find she is in a coma again and can't talk, can't see or hear.

Why didn't I tell her yesterday the important things I want say? What can I do?

So I whisper in her ear, hoping what I say will be heard in her subconscious, all I can say to her is, thank you for loving me unconditionally since the day we met.

You are the best thing that could have happened to me, and hope she heard me.

I don't put makeup on her today.

I called all the family to get down and prepare themselves to see her for the final time.

While waiting for them, and before deciding if I would make that final decision, I was thinking, do I trust these doctors?

I again think, have I been selfish keeping her alive, I know she would keep fighting as long as I asked her to, but is it right for her. I wonder do other people second guess themselves like this?

My mind wanders again while waiting.

Her one disappointment in life was that neither of her sons had found true love and a long term marriage.

The elder son, against our wishes married too young, had bought her 2 grand children from that marriage.

It had only survived a few years and he had not been able to find any one since that time who he wanted to marry.

He had many girl friends but none who Margie could or wanted to call a daughter in law.

Margie didn't meet his current wife until the week she got ill, at least she met her once.

They did marry and have had four children, and it disappoints me that she did not get to know her new daughter in law and her grand children.

I know she would have idealised and spoilt them all.

Our youngest son, who broke up with his first long term girlfriend , his true love at his 21st birthday.

The girl Margie wanted him to marry and who he should have married as far as we were concerned, and to this day he agrees was his biggest mistake.

Working in Melbourne he met a city girl, against our advice married too young.

Why do parents know these things?

Margie didn't want it to happen, she didn't think the marriage would survive, and it didn't.

She wasn't wrong many times.

We didn't go to the wedding by mutual agreement with the bride even though it broke her heart not to be part of it

She stood by her conviction no matter even if it hurt her,

Not speaking to her son for 12 months after was also heart breaking for her..

It had only lasted 12 months; there was no I told you so, just relief she had her son back and a granddaughter as a bonus.

The short marriage together had produced a daughter that he has raised basically on his own, and who Margie had also looked after as a baby and really loved.

He then met a country girl that we liked and hoped could lead to marriage but she had personal family troubles and took her own life, which devastated him and affected us all.

He then met yet another country girl we thought could be the right one that marriage.

Sadly it only last a few years and finished a few months before she became ill, we had known for some time it could not survive.

I whispered to her that youngest son had finally made arrangements to meet his old flame on a date and maybe her wishes might come finally true.

I knew that would make her happy, I was hoping she could hear.

She would have been proud of her two older granddaughters who have grown to be beautiful young women. She would be pleased with what they have done with their life so far, and what they will do with their life.

It also disappoints me she was not here as she wanted to be, to advise them, to be part of their last teen years, their school proms, their 21st birthdays, meeting their first loves, getting married and then their children.

The time finally arrives to make that fateful decision, her vital signs and oxygen saturations are not good and I finally agree with the doctors after all her family have had time to see and talk to her, to turn off her life support.

This was the hardest decision, I will ever make in my life, only those who have had to do it will understand.

Its 7.20 pm, How did things change from yesterday is running through my mind.

I left the room and my youngest son Rod stayed with

her and this was the most important thing that could have happened for her.

Suddenly, she came out of the coma, she had tears in her eyes and he would be the last person she would see as he wiped the tears from her eyes, and his voice was the last voice she would hear, saying, I love you mum, go to sleep mummy, I will look after Dad and Scott.

By the time I got back in to the room minutes later she was gone.

As I held her in my arms and kissed her for the final time I remembered those vows we said to each other on that Friday night so many years ago, "until till death do us part", we had certainly kept our word to each other.

I wished I had been the last person she saw, but I'm happy that one of the people she loved was there when she opened her eyes for the last time.

We both believed your spirit stays when you die, after reading many stories about it, so I look to the ceiling while holding her and tell her,

I promise I will find the truth of what happened and get justice for you, and I will always love you.

I can only hope she heard me.

We all need to believe in something.

She had put up a massive fight and shown unbelievable courage to survive the last 21 days but in the end the damage done to her by incompetent and negligent doctors was too much.

She is now another victim of medical negligence and malpractice, but I will get the answers.

The incorrect insertion of the central vein cannulation, the incorrect insertion of the wire into the femoral artery, was not done on purpose.

They are known foreseeable risks for the procedures, but they were negligent mistakes because nothing was done by the doctors to mitigate the known risks which would be to simply, use a doppler ultrasound to assist in placing the cannula in the right place.

The crime is, when doctors and hospitals refuse to admit the mistakes and then collude to cover up the mistakes. putting lives at more risk by failing to rectify the mistake when it was possible.

Their refusal to acknowledge the mistakes they had made to me when I saw her that night when I asked how her lung collapsed demonstrated the intent to hide the mistakes.

The truth then, would have enabled me to use my legal right to transfer her immediately to a major Melbourne hospital where vascular surgeons could have repaired the torn artery, which would have saved her life.

And more importantly, saved her 21 days of unnecessary trauma.

The cover-up is worse than the crime or mistake.

Medicine is a science of the human body and mistakes can happen.

We need to accept that fact, but not forget that doctors and general hospitals even aged care hospitals owe patients an absolute duty of care on how they administer that responsibility.

There are brilliant doctors and dedicated nurses in the medical industry as were the nurses at that trauma hospital ICU who managed Margie's progress, also there are those who aren't and who don't have that ability and if you get one of the not so brilliant your life or your family member's life can be in danger.

An example would be the night shift ICU HMO in the early hours of the morning at the country hospital.

So concerned with her condition and the colour of her limb he attempted to find an arterial doppler to check blood flow to the limb and when he couldn't get one, he showed initiative.

He found another surgeon unrelated to the case to look at Margie and give an opinion on the limb.

And it was that competent surgeon who made the

decision at 5am that her condition was serious enough to arrange transfer to a Melbourne hospital and took control of her management, albeit too late to save the limb.

CHAPTER TWENTY

Twenty minutes after turning off life support her life is gone, I was proud of her for not giving up, but the fight begins for me to find out WHY.

She had loved me unconditionally since the day we met and her life was not completed through no fault of hers.

It's not until they are gone you realise the things you didn't say to them, now it's too late and you will regret it.

We now go from negligent damages claim, to a wrongful death claim. The claim would get some media attention after it was filed.

But first I have to challenge the cause of death and have the erroneous death certificate changed.

It would take me 2 years to get the Coroner to agree with my cause of death, which was septicemia of the leg wound and the small intestines not a cop-out organ failure as the hospital wanted on the certificate.

As many people know the first time you walk in the door of your home after the funeral is an unreal feeling, no matter how comfortable the house was, it's now a cold empty place of loneliness.

I advise people not to just accept what happens, but to fight for the victim or yourself, to get justice.

I had learnt to never let a lawyer have complete control or carte blanche over a matter.

That mistake had cost us thousands of dollars with incompetent lawyers over the years.

I went back to work driving but it's hard to drive a truck when all you have is time to think and it's hard to see where you are going with eyes that won't stop watering

I issued a freedom of information demand on the Melbourne trauma hospital for her complete files and I found lawyers who will work with me to see justice done for her wrongful death.

You find out that, according to the opinions of insurance companies and the law that when people reach 70, and not a breadwinner, their life is deemed over and useless.

You also learn that truth and justice in a court of law have no place in civil litigation, once lawyers get involved justice is the last resort they take.

It's all about the money, and going to court for truth or Justice is too risky.

I now have the challenge to learn and understand a thousand pages of medical records.

At the same time, study medical malpractice law so that I can understand any breaches of law that were committed by doctors or the hospitals.

That study would help get me the diploma of law I needed so that I can have some form of input to any action I take through these lawyers.

I learnt that proper and fair compensation is hard and sometimes impossible to get for that older age person.

The first thing you learn from her files from the Melbourne hospital is why her vitals an saturations went from good to bad on that final night.

Her files show that the particular drugs she had been on to keep her alive were not given to her after midnight, and not administered on that final day, all without my consent.

But without an autopsy, that can't be proven. The doctors had gotten their way and pulled the plug on her life.

I should have demanded an autopsy when they refused

my request for one so I found out even good doctors make mistakes.

People have to understand if they don't like what has happened to their family member or themselves ask questions, and the first thing is get copies of all hospital records and read them.

Reading her files from her time at the regional country hospital where she was first admitted, show the panic and the incompetence over a 10 minute time line of mistakes.

From when they inserted the line in the wrong place for a Central Vein cannulation in the chest, that is when they punctured the left lung, causing cardiac arrest.

To the next mistake, while the patient is in cardiac arrest and they are panicking, is trying to do a femoral artery cannulation to make up for the previous mistake without mitigating the risk by using arterial doppler assistance, which lead to the tearing of the femoral artery causing a major blockage of the artery.

Finally, by failing to notice the limb is becoming ischemic.

(There is question whether they did notice the necrosis but did nothing about it)

Then, compounding those mistakes with not bothering to use a doppler to check blood flow after the leg started going Ischemic in colour 5 minutes after the procedure.

Chapter twenty

You find all this out by studying the medical files.

The nominated surgeon put in charge of her said he would check in on her the morning.

The afternoon ICU HMO was past his knock off time, and left her management to a trainee doctor and nurses.

Intensive Care means dedicated minute by minute nursing, except in that regional country hospital and other country hospitals that doesn't apply.

The surgeon who was in charge of her management in that regional hospital lost all and any credibility when he said in a management hearing "I decided not to transfer her for vascular surgery because in my opinion she wouldn't survive the flight to the Melbourne hospital", showed he knew the leg was ischemic at 7pm .

The fact her condition 12 hours later was 50% worse than that time, and the fact she survived the transfer showed his judgment had no basis of medical fact, and his decision was clouded by his support for his associates involved in her flawed management in the ICU, and is the reason why doctors don't, and shouldn't have, the ultimate right to make life or death decisions, and must be held accountable for their action or non action.

The right to decide whether or not to transfer a patient for better care lies with the patient or family, not the doctors or hospital administrators.

And had they told me the truth that evening I would have demanded she be sent to a major capital city hospital as per my right in law.

What every person in charge at that hospital failed to act on was saving her limbs.

Following a period of 6 hours without blood supply to the limbs causes necrosis to our limbs and they are slowly dying, and can't be saved, which is common in car and industrial accidents.

The final insult was, had that I had known who the surgeon in charge of her management was I would have sought other opinions

She had seen him in his private practice and had called him an arrogant prick and would not go back to see him again.

The surgeon's argument to me that it was a small country hospital and there are no vascular surgeons in the hospital who could rectify the torn artery.

That statement turned out to be the statement that would turn the case and bring them undone.

There were many grounds in the final writ for wrongful death against the hospital and the doctors involved for gross negligence and incompetence.

But to me the evidence turned on an opinion of a professor of surgery procedures that her lawyers find as an expert, who said, surgeons can specialize in any field.

Another clothes modeling job

However they are first and foremost surgeons and any competent surgeon is qualified in an emergency to perform any surgery, in this case, to repair a torn artery.

There are many competent surgeons in that country town who could have been asked,

The word competent highlighted in the case of the surgeon who was attending to her management that night.

She could have been operated on that night immediately the leg showed to be ischemic, and had they repaired the artery she would be alive today,

It was clear to me that, after reading her file, they never expected her to survive the night.

They would have covered up their mistakes, by saying she died of pneumonia during the night, and we would never have known what actually happened, but she was a fighter.

One wonders how often this is done.

The intervention of that passing surgeon in the early hours of the morning checking on his own patient who was asked his opinion on her leg was crucial,

His action to check the artery and arrange the hospital transfer, did, I believe, unknowingly prevent the mistakes known to the other doctors involved in her management that were not known to others, and prevented the cover-up from being effective and saved her from dying that night.

CHAPTER TWENTY ONE

Four years to the date of her funeral the hospital settled the wrongful death claim at a court ordered mediation, without wanting to test the evidence at trial as I wanted.

I am confident and I will always believe, had it gone to trial it could have been proven that she was killed by incompetence, negligence, cover-up and bias toward elderly patients.

That there was conspiracy in an effort to cover up her mismanagement by those doctors entrusted to look after her.

She has the justice I promised her that night she died.

The four year fight to keep the promise had got me through depression after her death.

And at the same time a 3 year fight to beat prostate cancer, and a hip replacement.

Even in her death she kept me alive and writing this story of her life has helped me out of the depression of losing her.

The feeling of walking into our house the night the action was settled was worse than the feeling I had coming home from the funeral, emptiness

It is now time to live without her and let her go.

I would take a cruise a couple of years later and would have a picture of her under my jacket, and enjoy a waltz on the promenade deck under the stars, just as she would have liked to have done.

I knew the professional dancers on the ship and I asked one of them if she would dance slow fox trot with me on the main dance floor,

I visualized it was Margie, that whole scene would have been straight out a movie for her.

I know that the remainder of my life living on my own will be hard; I don't expect any other woman to want to take her place. And I have photos and memories, no thanks to these negligent doctors and hospital.

The problem I have now is I see her everywhere and I'm constantly being reminded of her and how she looked, as I see her in the actress's on TV shows and in movies.

I see in my mind this beautiful woman with her blonde hair, her golden tanned body lying on the beach, beads of water on her stomach from swimming, just enjoying the sun and life.

The photos of family are good memories, and it's when I look at some photos of her that my mind goes back to what I used to tell her, that the female body, her body, was the 8th wonder of the world. So perfect.

Her message that still resonates with me while writing her story is:

Attention to detail, Jerry.
If a job is worth doing its worth doing properly

Time doesn't dim memories, or the guilt about whether I, should I have amputated the leg if it would have saved her from the pain of fighting ,Could I have done better, Maybe a different hospital, or been taken to hospital sooner, Could I have given her a better life, loved her more?

Answer is probably, but at the time they were the right things to do.

But the disappointment that she is not here to share in the rewards of all those hard years is difficult to take.

We could have been constantly on holidays enjoying those tropical islands she so adored and loved

I have tried doing it on my own, it's not the same.

It's hard to hide the jealousy you feel seeing other couples enjoying life ,young couples who don't know how quick life can change and older couples, still together who might never understand what they have. You feel you should tell them not to waste any time they have left.

Only 2 weeks before she got ill I had told her I was retiring from long distance driving and I would stay home. We would renew our vows, and we could enjoy a proper honey moon.

She was so excited and looking forward to doing it. More regrets, that we didn't get to spend that time together.

Spontaneous gifts and surprises, she loved it.

If I see a nice dress in the window when walking past women's clothing shops I have to stop myself thinking she would lovely in that and buying it, like I used to.

Especially if it was blue .

The surprise look and pleasure on her face when I came home with a dress is worth remembering.

On birthdays and special days I would look for perfumes she would like or I would buy her lingerie, her reaction upon receiving them was all the reward I needed and priceless.

I remember seeing a light blue silk full length negligee one time with slits down both sides from the arm pits to the bottom with one simple silk tie string at the waist.

I couldn't buy it quick enough and give it to her, true Hollywood she said.

When she wore that to bed she could have been straight out of a movie.

She always said, when it comes to clothes woman should remember the adage more can be less, leaving things to the imagination can be more alluring. It's how you use what you have. Wearing dresses that let boobs fall out or show your bum does not necessarily do that, although, that's not what modern society believes.

She had class; I compare her to Lauren Bacall, who in my opinion was one of the classy ladies of Hollywood. And contrary to what women of today believe, having money and or living in a mansion doesn't make you classy.

It's how you conduct yourself with others irrespective of money or your address that show your real class as a woman or person.

She also loved the message it sent to other women when walking down the street arm in arm, holding hands or me putting my arm around her waist, the message? He's mine.

They say that it's up men to make their partner feel protected when they embrace them and rightly so, But to me, the role changed.

A simple hug or embrace from her every day gave me a feeling of protection and strength, I miss that every day.

CHAPTER 22

I was asked to look at another patients file from that regional hospital after they died and the evidence showed the true cause of death was covered up, notes and records altered, sadly evidence was lost from the file.

It was past the statute of limitations to take action by the family, so the family couldn't act on it.

It happens only too often by this country hospital and some other hospitals. I can only imagine how often families must be put I similar positions.

I recommend that people don't just accept what they are told by doctors or hospitals question everything, and if you have doubts, obtain their medical records and read them as soon as they are released from hospital.

Medical malpractice is one the hardest areas of law to litigate because you need to argue against a doctor which is a professional opinion.

The doctor is basically an expert, and a layman's opinion doesn't carry any weight.

You find that doctors don't want to assist you in helping to win against one of their own.

The evidence needed to win will be in the hospital records, and medical malpractice precedents, local, and across the world, and the special doctor's that experienced lawyers find that do care what mistakes are being done and who will speak out.

Everyone who watches the medical shows on television where the doctors and nurses are magicians, they never make mistakes and only have the patient's health on their minds as a priority.

No matter what their age or illness everyone in the management of the patient treats them like they are their family member.

We expect and hope, I know I do, that our doctors and nurses will be the same when we need them.

It does happen, but only in a perfect world would that happen all the time and ours is far from it

We know death is part of life and we all hope it won't happen to us until we are ready for it.

Chapter 22

However we have no control over that and we hope that the doctors we go to will do their best to prolong that life.

In true life, in every vocation, there are the brilliant and dedicated, and then those who are just ordinary.

Then there are those who will take whatever steps it takes to protect their mistakes, lack of ability, and or dedication to the profession they are in.

But to the doctors and management involved at *t*hat regional country hospital *Margie* has never existed, no remorse was ever offered from the doctors involved or the management of the hospital to *Margie's* family, except a half hearted sorry, and that doesn't help her or me.

Everyone has those moments when we say, I'd like to go back in time and know what I know now.

I can say, our lives we would be different if I could do that

I finally now ask myself the question again, was I selfish trying to keep her alive knowing she wouldn't have quality of life by amputating her leg.

I answer myself, yes, but I justify it by saying she wouldn't have been alone had she survived; but I still have to wonder if that would have really been the best quality of life for her.

Margaret Leah Brown was a romantic and always thought her life was romantic and perfect.

She wanted to write book about it to share with others but couldn't find the time.

Her story had she written it, would have had a happy ending unlike this one.

I know she would have written it different to me, because this is a story of her life, and including her untimely death as I remember it.

This book is dedicated to *Margie,* my wife

She was the perfect woman, the perfect wife, the perfect mother. And also, She was a lady and my best friend

www.ingramcontent.com/pod-product-compliance
Lightning Source LLC
Chambersburg PA
CBHW021114080526
44587CB00010B/511